FORAGING

FOR

BEGINNERS

DR. KIMBERLY CARLOS

Copyright © 2023 by Dr. Kimberly Carlos

All rights reserved. No part of this publication may be reproduced, distributed, or transmitted in any form or by any means, including photocopying, recording, or other electronic or mechanical methods, without the prior written permission of the publisher, except in the case of brief quotations embodied in critical reviews and certain other noncommercial uses permitted by copyright law.

TABLE OF CONTENT

CHAPTER ONE

The Fascinating World of Foraging

The enchanting call of the wild, echoing through the dense, untouched landscapes, beckons us to reconnect with our primal instincts and rediscover a world brimming with untamed bounty. In an age where supermarket shelves are stacked high with neatly packaged produce and pre-processed foods, the art of foraging harkens back to a time when humans depended on the land and nature's harvests for sustenance. It is a practice as ancient as humanity itself, etched into our genetic memory, and yet, for many, it remains a largely uncharted territory, waiting to be explored.

Imagine a leisurely walk through a sun-dappled forest, your eyes scanning the undergrowth for a hidden treasure trove of edible delights. The feeling of discovery, the thrill of uncovering the freshest, most vibrant flavors nature has to offer, is an experience unlike any other. This is the heart and soul of foraging - a journey of culinary exploration, a communion with the natural world, and a profound connection to our roots.

In this modern age, foraging for food is not just a means of sustenance; it has become a movement, a way of life, and a celebration of sustainable living. The art of foraging not only nourishes our bodies but also nurtures our souls. It reconnects us with the land, fostering a deep appreciation for the cycles of life, the seasons, and the intricate web of life that supports us all. The simple act of foraging encourages us to slow down, to listen to the whispers of the wind and the rustling of leaves, and to observe the subtle changes in the natural world around us.

This book, "Foraging for Beginners," is your key to unlocking the mysteries and magic of foraging. In its pages, we will embark on an extraordinary journey together, exploring the bountiful and diverse offerings of the wild, from the verdant forests and meadows to the tranquil shores and clear streams. We will delve into the practical aspects of foraging, such as the tools you need, the safety guidelines to follow, and the essential knowledge to distinguish edible treasures from their potentially hazardous counterparts.

But foraging is more than just a means to an end; it is a journey of wonderment. It's about embracing the rhythms of nature, understanding the plants and fungi that provide us with nourishment, and forging a deeper connection with the earth and its rhythms. You'll discover the stories and history of these remarkable plants and organisms, their culinary and medicinal uses, and the role they've played in human civilization for centuries.

Our exploration will extend beyond the act of foraging itself. We will learn how to savor these newfound treasures by preparing delectable dishes that bring out the best of each ingredient. We'll explore various preservation methods to ensure the joy of foraging can be extended throughout the year, and even share ways in which foraging can be a stepping stone to self-sufficiency and sustainability.

As we journey through the pages of this book, you'll come to understand that foraging is more than just a survival skill; it's a gateway to a deeper, more meaningful relationship with nature. It's a way of nourishing not only our bodies but also our spirits, grounding us in a world teeming with beauty, abundance, and wonder. So, let us embark on this enchanting voyage, guided by the whispers of the wild, and discover the fascinating world of foraging together.

The Timeless Art of Foraging

Foraging, the age-old practice of gathering food and resources from the wild, is an art as ancient as humanity itself. Long before the advent of agriculture, supermarkets, and modern conveniences, our ancestors relied on the land's offerings to meet their basic needs. In this ever-changing world, the art of foraging remains a timeless and essential skill that connects us to our roots, sustains us, and offers a glimpse into the history of human survival.

The roots of foraging can be traced back to a time when human existence was intrinsically tied to the natural world. Our ancestors, hunter-gatherers, roamed vast landscapes, searching for nourishment. They depended on the bounty of the land, from edible plants and fruits to nuts, mushrooms, and a variety of animals. Foraging was not merely a means of survival; it was a way of life, a practice that fostered a deep understanding of the land, its cycles, and the ecological interplay that sustained life.

In the modern era, the allure of foraging is stronger than ever. In an age marked by concerns about food security, environmental sustainability, and a growing disconnection from nature, foraging offers a way to return to our roots and find solace in the natural world. It encourages us to step outside the confines of our fast-paced, technology-driven lives and reconnect with the Earth. There's a profound sense of peace that comes from strolling through the woods, scanning the underbrush, and uncovering the hidden treasures of nature. The timelessness of foraging is mirrored in its resilience and adaptability. From the dawn of human civilization to the present day, foraging has been a common thread weaving through different cultures and geographies. Indigenous communities around the world have developed unique foraging practices, passing down knowledge through generations. Whether it's the Native American tradition of gathering wild rice or the Scandinavian custom of hunting for mushrooms, foraging persists as an enduring practice, a testament to its enduring appeal.

In a world where the origins of our food are often obscured by factory farming, foraging offers a direct and transparent connection to what we consume. It is the ultimate form of organic and sustainable eating. Foragers take only what they need and, in doing so, participate in a natural rhythm that allows the land to regenerate. It is an act of reciprocity, a give-and-take relationship with the earth. When we forage responsibly, we become stewards of the land, ensuring the perpetuity of its gifts.

The art of foraging transcends mere sustenance; it is a profound connection with the world around us. The act of identifying, harvesting, and preparing wild foods is a journey of discovery. It requires keen observation, a deep understanding of ecosystems, and an appreciation for the intricacies of each plant, fungi, or creature encountered. Every foraging expedition becomes an opportunity to learn, to connect with nature's wonders, and to appreciate the astonishing variety of flavors and textures that the wild provides.

The timelessness of foraging also extends to its role as a bridge between generations. The knowledge of foraging, passed down from elders to younger generations, maintains a cultural continuity that links us to our heritage. It is a living tradition, reminding us of the wisdom contained in the experiences of our ancestors and the importance of preserving these age-old practices for the future.

In a world driven by convenience and speed, foraging stands as a testament to the enduring connection between humanity and the land that sustains us. It is a practice that nourishes not only our bodies but also our souls, offering a profound sense of unity with the natural world. The timeless art of foraging beckons us to step outside, to slow down, and to partake in the boundless, ever-giving banquet of the Earth. It is a call to honor our past, embrace the present, and secure a sustainable future—one harvest at a time.

The Joy of Connecting with Nature

In a fast-paced and increasingly urbanized world, the joy of connecting with nature is a precious and essential experience. It is a reminder of our deep-seated connection to the natural world and the profound impact it has on our physical, mental, and emotional well-being. Whether we find solace in the forest, serenity by the sea, or wonder in a garden, the act of immersing ourselves in nature is a source of joy that transcends cultures and generations.

When we speak of the joy of connecting with nature, we are acknowledging a fundamental human need—an instinctual yearning for the outdoors. This desire is imprinted in our DNA, a heritage from our ancestors who once roamed vast landscapes, attuned to the rhythms of the natural world. When we heed this primal call and venture into nature, we discover a sense of belonging and harmony, an opportunity to return to a place where we are not just observers, but participants.

One of the most profound joys of connecting with nature is the unburdening of our daily stresses. In a world filled with the ceaseless noise of traffic, the blare of screens, and the hustle of urban life, nature serves as a refuge for our weary minds. The cacophony of modern existence is replaced by the gentle rustling of leaves, the songs of birds, and the soothing sounds of flowing water. This natural symphony offers a tranquility that is nothing short of therapeutic. In nature, we find not just peace but a sense of serenity that rejuvenates our spirits and restores balance to our lives.

Beyond the serenity, nature also stirs a sense of wonder and awe. The sheer diversity and beauty of the natural world are breathtaking. Whether it's witnessing the vibrant colors of a sunset, the intricate designs of a spider's web, or the delicate dance of a butterfly, nature captivates us with its artistry. The joy of connecting with nature lies in the moments of revelation, the "aha" moments when we realize the beauty, complexity, and elegance of the world around us.

Nature also provides a sense of timelessness and continuity. When we step into the wilderness or stroll through a historic garden, we connect with the past, present, and future all at once. The ancient trees, the timeless mountains, and the flowing rivers have borne witness to countless generations. Our actions and experiences become a part of this timeless tapestry, creating a sense of transcendence that few other experiences can provide.

The joy of connecting with nature also extends to our physical well-being. Time spent outdoors, whether hiking, cycling, or simply taking leisurely walks, promotes fitness and a healthier lifestyle. Breathing fresh, clean air and engaging in physical activity amidst the beauty of nature can significantly improve our physical health and mental vitality. It's a reminder that our bodies are meant to move and thrive in the great outdoors.

Furthermore, our connection with nature encourages environmental consciousness. As we immerse ourselves in natural landscapes, we develop a greater understanding of the delicate balance of ecosystems and our place within them. This understanding fosters a sense of responsibility and a desire to protect the very environments that bring us so much joy.

The joy of connecting with nature is also a powerful antidote to the growing epidemic of nature-deficit disorder, especially among children. Time spent in nature helps young minds develop creativity, curiosity, and a deep appreciation for the world around them. It kindles a sense of adventure and wonder that can last a lifetime.

In a world teeming with the latest gadgets and distractions, the joy of connecting with nature is a reminder of what truly matters. It's an opportunity to escape the relentless demands of modern life, rekindle our spirits, and find solace in the natural world. It is a connection to the past, a celebration of the present, and an investment in the future. Nature, in all its majesty, beckons us to experience the profound joy of connecting with the world that sustains us.

Benefits of Foraging for Food and Health

Foraging, the age-old practice of gathering food from the wild, offers a cornucopia of benefits for both physical well-being and mental health. While modern society has largely moved away from this primal skill in favor of supermarkets and convenience foods, the rewards of foraging for food and health are a compelling reason to embrace this ancient art.

1. Nutrient-Rich Food: Wild foraged foods are often more nutrient-dense than their cultivated counterparts. Foragers have access to a diverse array of plant species, each offering a unique combination of vitamins, minerals, and antioxidants. From wild berries bursting with vitamin C to foraged greens packed with essential nutrients, these natural foods contribute to a healthier and more balanced diet.

2. Variety of Flavors: Foraging introduces individuals to an exciting array of flavors that are not commonly found in traditional grocery stores. The rich and diverse tastes of wild edibles can enliven culinary experiences, making meals more interesting and enjoyable. It's a journey into the world of gastronomic diversity, where each plant or fungus tells its own flavorful story.

3. Sustainable and Local Sourcing: Foraging is the epitome of local and sustainable sourcing. By gathering food directly from nature, foragers reduce the carbon footprint associated with conventional agriculture, transportation, and packaging. This practice contributes to environmental sustainability and a lower impact on the planet.

4. Increased Physical Activity: Foraging often involves physical activity, such as hiking, bending, and squatting, as foragers search for hidden treasures in the wilderness. This physical engagement is a natural way to boost fitness and burn calories, helping individuals stay active and maintain a healthy weight.

5. Mental Well-Being: The act of foraging in the great outdoors is a balm for the mind and soul. Spending time in nature has been linked to reduced stress, anxiety, and depression. The sights, sounds, and smells of the natural world have a calming and restorative effect, fostering mental clarity and emotional well-being.

6. Mindful Connection to Nature: Foraging is a practice that encourages a deep and mindful connection to the environment. It requires keen observation, patience, and respect for the ecosystems that provide our food. This mindfulness cultivates an appreciation for the beauty and complexity of nature, promoting a sense of serenity and interconnectedness.

7. Culinary Creativity: Foragers often find themselves experimenting in the kitchen, incorporating wild ingredients into their culinary creations. This culinary creativity not only results in delicious and unique dishes but also provides a sense of satisfaction and accomplishment.

8. Resilience and Self-Sufficiency: Foraging is a skill that can be developed and passed down through generations. It equips individuals with the knowledge to find food in the wild, which can be invaluable in survival situations. The self-sufficiency gained from foraging is empowering and fosters a sense of resilience.

9. Community Building: Foraging can be a communal activity, bringing people together to explore and appreciate the natural world. Sharing knowledge and experiences with others builds a sense of community and strengthens social bonds.

10. Medicinal and Herbal Knowledge: Foraging extends beyond food to encompass medicinal and herbal plants. Many wild plants have therapeutic properties and can be used in natural remedies. Foragers can acquire a wealth of knowledge about the healing properties of various plants, enhancing their health and well-being.

It's important to note that foraging should be approached with care and responsibility. Proper plant identification is essential to avoid accidental ingestion of toxic species, and foraging should be done in a sustainable manner to protect the environment. However, with the right guidance and a commitment to ethical foraging practices, individuals can tap into the incredible benefits of foraging for food and health.

Foraging offers a holistic approach to food and health. It is a journey of nourishment, a connection to nature, and an exploration of flavors and nutrients that enrich our lives. By foraging responsibly, individuals can enjoy the myriad benefits that this timeless practice has to offer, all while fostering a deeper appreciation for the natural world that surrounds us.

The Ethical and Sustainable Aspects of Foraging

Foraging is not only a means of connecting with nature and obtaining fresh, nutritious food; it is also a practice rooted in ethics and sustainability. This ancient art, when conducted responsibly, can contribute to the conservation of ecosystems and promote a harmonious relationship between humans and the environment. The ethical and sustainable aspects of foraging underscore the importance of understanding, respecting, and nurturing the ecosystems from which we gather our wild edibles.

1. Respect for Ecosystems: Responsible foraging begins with a profound respect for the ecosystems in which it takes place. Foragers recognize that they are visitors in nature's domain, and they approach their activities with a deep appreciation for the delicate balance of life within these ecosystems. Understanding the interconnectedness of all living things is essential to ethical foraging.

2. Plant Identification: Ethical foragers prioritize proper plant identification. They invest time in learning to distinguish edible plants from potentially harmful ones. Misidentification can have serious consequences for both individuals and ecosystems. Ethical foragers consult field guides, experts, and local knowledge to ensure they gather only safe and sustainable resources.

3. Harvesting Practices: Ethical foragers adopt sustainable harvesting practices. They collect wild edibles in a way that minimizes harm to the plants, fungi, and their surrounding environments. Techniques like selective harvesting, which involves taking only a portion of a plant or mushroom, help ensure the continued growth and vitality of the species.

4. Avoiding Overharvesting: Overharvesting is a common concern in foraging. Ethical foragers understand the importance of not depleting wild populations. They avoid harvesting in areas where species are scarce or already threatened. Some even participate in citizen science initiatives to monitor and protect vulnerable species.

5. Leave No Trace: The "leave no trace" principle is central to ethical foraging. This concept entails leaving the foraging area in the same or better condition than when it was found. Littering, trampling, and damage to ecosystems are strictly avoided. Ethical foragers carry out their harvests with utmost care, leaving nature undisturbed.

6. Preservation of Biodiversity: Ethical foraging supports biodiversity by promoting a diverse diet. Foragers understand that focusing on a single species can lead to overharvesting and depletion. They celebrate the diversity of wild edibles and work to preserve the ecosystems in which these species thrive.

7. Recognition of Native and Invasive Species: Ethical foragers recognize the impact of invasive species on native ecosystems. While they may harvest invasive species for food, they also understand the importance of controlling and managing these species to protect native flora and fauna.

8. Promotion of Sustainable Practices: Ethical foragers promote sustainable foraging practices within their communities. They share knowledge and experiences with others, educating them about the ethical and sustainable aspects of foraging. This awareness fosters a culture of responsible foraging that can have a positive impact on local ecosystems.

9. Legal Considerations: Ethical foragers are also mindful of the legal aspects of foraging. They are aware of regulations and restrictions in their foraging areas, obtaining necessary permits or permissions where required. Respecting legal guidelines ensures that foraging remains a sustainable and ethical practice.

10. Conservation Efforts: Many ethical foragers actively engage in conservation efforts to give back to the ecosystems that provide their sustenance. They participate in habitat restoration projects, volunteer with environmental organizations, and advocate for the protection of natural areas.

The ethical and sustainable aspects of foraging highlight the importance of forging a harmonious relationship with the natural world. It is not a one-sided endeavor of taking from the environment; rather, it is a reciprocal relationship in which foragers actively work to protect and preserve the ecosystems that provide for them. Ethical foraging is a manifestation of the deep respect and gratitude for the land and its gifts, reinforcing the idea that sustainability and the well-being of both humans and nature are inextricably linked.

By adhering to ethical and sustainable foraging practices, individuals can ensure that the time-honored tradition of gathering food from the wild can continue for generations to come, contributing to the preservation of our natural heritage and the health of our planet. In a world where environmental concerns are paramount, foraging offers a pathway to sustainability and a model for responsible coexistence with the ecosystems that sustain us.

CHAPTER TWO

Getting Started with Foraging

In the hustle and bustle of our modern lives, where the aisles of grocery stores offer a seemingly endless array of neatly packaged and processed foods, it's easy to overlook the bountiful treasures that the natural world provides. Yet, beneath the surface of manicured lawns, lush meadows, dense forests, and pristine shorelines lies an untamed wilderness teeming with edible wonders. Foraging, the age-old practice of gathering food from the wild, is a call to reconnect with this often-forgotten source of sustenance and rediscover a world where the land itself provides for our nourishment.

The journey into the enchanting realm of foraging begins with the realization that we have within us an innate connection to the natural world—a connection that has been buried beneath layers of concrete and convenience. In the act of foraging, we rekindle this primal link and embark on an adventure that transcends the mere procurement of sustenance; it is a journey of discovery, an exploration of the senses, and a profound connection with the Earth.

This serves as your guide to this remarkable expedition into the wilds of nature. Within its pages, you will find the knowledge, tools, and inspiration to begin your own foraging journey. We will explore the essentials of foraging, from the basic equipment you'll need to the safety guidelines that will ensure your foraging experience remains enjoyable and secure. The journey begins by understanding the tools of the trade, such as field guides, baskets, and pocket knives, and learning to navigate the terrain you'll explore.

But foraging is more than just a utilitarian endeavor. It's a voyage of discovery, a journey into the heart of the land that sustains us, and an awakening of the senses. In the chapters that follow, you'll learn to identify and appreciate the myriad edible treasures that the wild offers. From vibrant greens and alluring wildflowers to succulent berries and elusive fungi, each step in your foraging journey will reveal the diverse and delectable world of wild foods.

Foraging is not merely an art of gathering; it's a practice of reverence and understanding. In the wilderness, you'll find an assortment of ecosystems, each with its own unique array of species, interactions, and stories. As you embark on your foraging adventures, you'll become an observer of nature, learning to recognize the plants and fungi, their life cycles, and their role within the ecosystem. You'll come to understand the delicate dance of the seasons, the importance of biodiversity, and the interconnectedness of all life.

To get started with foraging is to tap into a sustainable and ecologically responsible way of nourishing yourself. In an age marked by concerns about overexploitation, industrial agriculture, and environmental degradation, foraging offers an opportunity to partake in a more intimate and conscientious relationship with the land. It encourages us to take only what we need, to respect the rhythms of nature, and to engage in a reciprocal exchange with the Earth, where we give back as much as we take.

In the pages that follow, we'll explore the diversity of edible plants, mushrooms, and other wild edibles that await discovery. We'll delve into the intricate processes of harvesting, cleaning, and storing your foraged bounty. Then, we'll embark on culinary adventures, learning to transform your wild finds into exquisite dishes that capture the essence of the natural world. Whether it's crafting delectable salads from freshly foraged greens, infusing flavors with wild herbs, or preparing dishes that feature wild berries and mushrooms, your culinary repertoire will expand as you connect more deeply with the wild.

Foraging also offers the chance to extend the bounty of the land through preservation methods such as drying, freezing, and canning. This knowledge empowers you to enjoy the flavors of the wild year-round, providing a direct and sustainable link to the land.

To get started with foraging is to embark on a journey of discovery, connection, and self-reliance. It's an invitation to walk through the door of the wild and witness the wonders that nature has to offer. It is a commitment to becoming a steward of the land, preserving the timeless art of foraging for future generations.

As we venture further into the world of foraging, you'll come to understand that it is not only a skill but a way of life—a practice that fosters reverence for nature, appreciation for the gifts it provides, and a deep sense of interconnectedness. The journey begins with that first step into the wilderness, and this book is your trusted companion, guiding you through the wondrous world of foraging. So, let us embark on this enchanting expedition, where the land becomes our provider, our mentor, and our eternal wellspring of nourishment and wonder.

Essential Tools and Equipment for Foraging

Foraging is a time-honored practice that connects us with the natural world and provides an opportunity to gather food from the wild. To engage in this ancient art effectively and safely, it's essential to be equipped with the right tools and equipment. These tools serve as your companions on the foraging journey, aiding in plant identification, harvest, and even preparation. In this exploration, we will delve into the crucial tools and equipment you'll need to embark on your foraging adventures.

1. Field Guides: A reliable field guide is a forager's best friend. These books or digital resources are packed with valuable information on plant and mushroom identification. They typically include clear photographs, detailed descriptions, and essential information about each species. Foraging field guides are region-specific, as plant life varies by location. Choose a guide tailored to your geographic area for the most accurate identification.

2. Basket or Bag: A sturdy, breathable basket or bag is indispensable for carrying your foraged treasures. Baskets, often made of wicker, allow air to circulate, which helps keep harvested plants fresh. They also prevent plants from getting crushed, unlike plastic bags. A shoulder strap or handle makes transportation easier, leaving your hands free for harvesting.

3. Gloves: While some foraging can be done with bare hands, a pair of gloves is valuable, especially when handling plants with thorns, stinging nettles, or poisonous species. Gloves provide protection, allowing you to handle wild edibles confidently.

4. Knife or Scissors: A sharp, compact knife or a pair of scissors is essential for cleanly and safely harvesting plants. Use them to snip leaves, stems, or mushrooms. Opt for a folding knife, which is easy to carry and less likely to cause accidents.

5. Magnifying Glass: A magnifying glass can be incredibly helpful, particularly for inspecting small details on plants or mushrooms. It aids in finer identification, especially when you're dealing with species that have subtle differences.

6. Pruning Shears: Foraging often involves cutting thicker stems or woody parts of plants. Pruning shears or garden scissors with longer blades provide the strength and precision required for such tasks.

7. Map and Compass or GPS: Depending on your foraging location, a map and compass or a GPS device can be invaluable for navigation. It's easy to get disoriented in the woods or wilderness, and having the tools to find your way back is crucial.

8. First Aid Kit: Safety should always be a priority while foraging. Carrying a basic first aid kit with essentials like bandages, antiseptic wipes, and tweezers for removing splinters is a wise precaution.

9. Insect Repellent: In many foraging environments, insects can be a nuisance or even pose health risks. Carrying insect repellent helps prevent bites and stings.

10. Weather-Appropriate Gear: Dressing appropriately for the weather is vital. Depending on your location and the season, you may need sunscreen, a hat, rain gear, or warm clothing. Sturdy, comfortable footwear with good grip is essential for safe and comfortable foraging.

11. Collection Containers: Small containers or bags can be used to separate different types of foraged items, making organization and storage more manageable.

12. Paper and Pen: A small notebook or a few sheets of paper, along with a pen or pencil, can be helpful for taking notes on your foraging discoveries. You can jot down location, observations, and any other useful information.

13. Mobile Apps: Several mobile apps are designed to aid in plant and mushroom identification. They can be handy for on-the-spot verification of species.

14. Compassionate and Responsible Attitude: While not a physical tool, having a compassionate and responsible mindset is crucial. Ethical foraging practices, such as sustainable harvesting, leave-no-trace principles, and an awareness of local regulations, are vital for protecting the environment and ensuring that wild edibles remain abundant for future generations.

15. Knowledge: Perhaps the most crucial tool of all is knowledge. Take the time to educate yourself about the wild edibles in your area, including their seasonality, growth patterns, and potential look-alike species. Learn from experienced foragers, take classes, and always err on the side of caution when uncertain.

These tools and equipment represent the foundation of a successful foraging experience. While your exact needs may vary depending on the location and types of wild edibles you seek, a well-prepared forager is one who respects the environment, adheres to ethical practices, and maximizes safety and success in their quest for the treasures of the wild. With the right tools and knowledge, you'll be well-equipped to embark on a journey of discovery, connection with nature, and a deeper understanding of the bountiful offerings that the natural world provides.

Safety Guidelines for Foraging

Foraging, the art of gathering food from the wild, is a rewarding and enriching experience. It connects us with nature, offers an array of fresh, natural foods, and fosters a profound sense of self-sufficiency. However, foraging also carries potential risks, as the natural world can be unpredictable and unforgiving. To ensure a safe and enjoyable foraging experience, it is essential to follow a set of safety guidelines that not only protect you but also preserve the ecosystems you interact with.

1. Proper Plant Identification: The cornerstone of foraging safety is the correct identification of plants and mushrooms. Misidentification can lead to harmful or even fatal consequences. Invest time in learning to distinguish edible species from potentially toxic look-alikes. Rely on trusted field guides, experts, and local knowledge to ensure accurate identification.

2. Avoiding Poisonous Species: Some plants and fungi in the wild are toxic and can cause severe illness or death. Make it a golden rule never to ingest anything you're not absolutely certain of. When in doubt, err on the side of caution and refrain from consuming it.

3. Sampling: If you are trying a new wild edible for the first time, start with a small sample to ensure there are no allergic reactions or digestive issues. If all is well after a small tasting, then proceed with consuming more.

4. Responsible Harvesting: Avoid overharvesting and be selective in your collection. Responsible foragers follow ethical guidelines to ensure they don't deplete wild populations. Leave enough plants behind to allow for natural propagation.

5. Environmentally Friendly Practices: Always adhere to "leave no trace" principles. Minimize your impact on the environment by not trampling on plants, damaging habitats, or leaving behind litter. Treat the natural world with respect, and leave the landscape as you found it.

6. Seasonal Awareness: The edibility and safety of wild plants can vary with the seasons. A plant that's safe to eat at one point in its life cycle may be toxic at another. Understand the life cycles and growth stages of the species you forage to make informed decisions.

7. Location and Habitat: Be aware of where you are foraging and the specific ecosystem you are in. Different plants grow in different habitats, and some areas may be more prone to pollution or contamination. Stay clear of foraging near roadsides or industrial areas where plants can absorb toxins.

8. Protected and Endangered Species: Know the legal status of wild plants and whether they are protected or endangered in your area. Avoid foraging in areas where protected species are found to prevent harm to the environment and potential legal consequences.

9. Health and Allergies: Be mindful of any pre-existing health conditions or allergies that may affect your foraging experience. Some wild edibles can have interactions with medications or exacerbate certain health conditions.

10. Preparation and Cooking: Not all wild edibles are safe to eat in their raw state. Some may contain compounds that are only neutralized through cooking or processing. Research the specific preparation and cooking methods required for the plants or fungi you forage.

11. Observation of Surroundings: Be aware of your surroundings at all times. Watch out for hazards like slippery terrain, steep cliffs, or encounters with wildlife. Stay hydrated, carry essential safety equipment, and let someone know your foraging location and expected return time if you are venturing into remote areas.

12. Sun Protection: When foraging in sunny conditions, protect your skin from harmful UV radiation by wearing sunscreen, a wide-brimmed hat, and appropriate clothing.

13. Water Safety: If your foraging adventure takes you near water sources, be cautious and ensure your safety. Do not consume water from natural sources without purifying it to prevent waterborne illnesses.

14. Children and Beginners: If you're introducing children or beginners to foraging, pay extra attention to safety measures. Teach them proper identification, the importance of responsible foraging, and always supervise them closely.

15. Permits and Regulations: Before foraging in public lands or protected areas, check local regulations and obtain any required permits. Respect these rules to ensure your activities are sustainable and legal.

Foraging is a fulfilling and sustainable practice, but safety should always be a top priority. By adhering to these safety guidelines, you can enjoy the wonders of the wild while minimizing risks to yourself and the environment. Your foraging experiences will be more rewarding, informed, and secure, providing a deeper connection to the natural world and a rich harvest of wild edibles.

Identifying and Avoiding Poisonous Plants

Foraging for wild edibles can be a captivating and rewarding experience, but it carries inherent risks, especially when it comes to identifying and avoiding poisonous plants. Accurate plant identification is crucial for the safety of foragers, as misidentifying a toxic plant can lead to severe illness or even prove fatal. To embark on a safe foraging journey, it is essential to develop the skills and knowledge needed to distinguish edible plants from their harmful counterparts.

Importance of Identification

The key to safe foraging is the ability to recognize both edible and poisonous plants. While numerous wild edibles offer nourishment, there are also a variety of toxic species lurking in the same landscapes. In the world of botany, many plants share similar characteristics, which can lead to confusion for the untrained eye. This is why the significance of precise plant identification cannot be overstated.

Common Poisonous Plants

Several common poisonous plants are found throughout the world, and being able to identify them is vital. Some well-known poisonous plants include:

1. Poison Ivy (Toxicodendron radicans): Recognizable by its three-leaf clusters and ability to cause itchy rashes upon contact.

2. Poison Oak (Toxicodendron diversilobum): Resembles poison ivy but often has lobed or toothed leaves.

3. Poison Sumac (Toxicodendron vernix): Identified by its pinnately compound leaves, containing seven to thirteen leaflets.

4. Hemlock (Conium maculatum): Often mistaken for edible herbs like wild carrots or parsley, it has purplish spots on its stem and a musty odor.

5. Foxglove (Digitalis purpurea): Recognizable by its tall spikes of bell-shaped flowers; all parts are toxic.

6. Deadly Nightshade (Atropa belladonna): Distinctive for its dark purple, bell-shaped flowers and shiny black berries.

7. Jimsonweed (Datura stramonium): Characterized by large, trumpet-shaped white or purple flowers and spiky seed pods.

Guidelines for Identifying Poisonous Plants

1. Start with Field Guides: Invest in reliable field guides or use reputable online resources. Local guides are particularly valuable, as they cover the species common to your region.

2. Learn Plant Families: Many edible and poisonous plants belong to the same botanical families. Understanding the traits of these families can assist with identification. For instance, the Umbelliferae family includes some edible species like carrots and parsnips but also contains the highly toxic hemlock.

3. Develop Plant Identification Skills: Focus on recognizing key characteristics, such as leaf shape, color, size, stem type, growth patterns, and flowers or fruits. Photographs in field guides can help you compare features to the plants you encounter.

4. Use All Senses: Identify plants by more than just their appearance. Touch, smell, and taste can provide additional clues, but exercise caution when using taste and ensure you are certain of the plant's edibility.

5. Seek Expert Guidance: If in doubt about a plant's identity, consult with experienced foragers or local botanists. They can offer invaluable guidance and share their expertise.

Safety Practices

Identifying and avoiding poisonous plants is an essential aspect of foraging safety. Consider these additional safety practices:

1. Keep a Foraging Journal: Document your foraging experiences, including plant identification, locations, and observations. This journal can serve as a reference for future forays.

2. Stay Informed: Stay updated on plant identification and safety practices. Botanical knowledge evolves, and it's essential to continue learning.

3. Forage Responsibly: Adhere to ethical foraging principles. Only take what you intend to use, and be selective to avoid overharvesting.

4. Keep Children Informed: If foraging with children, teach them about the dangers of poisonous plants and ensure they understand not to touch or ingest any plant without your guidance.

5. Avoid Consuming Unfamiliar Plants: Until you are confident in your plant identification skills, avoid consuming any wild plants, even if they resemble known edibles.

6. Wash Hands Thoroughly: After handling any plants in the wild, whether edible or not, thoroughly wash your hands to prevent any potential cross-contamination.

Identifying and avoiding poisonous plants is a fundamental aspect of responsible foraging. The ability to discern between safe and harmful species is a skill that ensures your foraging adventures are not only enjoyable but also secure. With dedication, practice, and ongoing learning, you can embark on a journey through nature's bounty, savoring the delights it offers while minimizing risks to your health.

Finding Suitable Foraging Locations

The search for suitable foraging locations is a critical aspect of the foraging journey. It involves identifying the right environments that offer a diverse array of wild edibles, as well as ensuring that foraging is conducted ethically, legally, and sustainably. To find the best foraging spots, one must embark on a quest that combines knowledge, observation, and a deep appreciation for the natural world.

1. Local Knowledge: Local knowledge is a treasure trove for foragers. People who have lived in an area for years often possess valuable insights about the best foraging locations, the seasons in which certain plants or fungi are abundant, and the rules and regulations governing foraging in their region. Engaging with local communities can provide a wealth of information.

2. Botanical Zones: Familiarize yourself with the botanical zones and ecosystems of your region. Different plant species thrive in specific environments. Coastal regions may offer seaweed and beach greens, while forests are rich in mushrooms, wild berries, and edible herbs. Understanding the ecosystems around you will guide you to the right locations.

3. Biodiversity Hotspots: Biodiversity hotspots are areas known for their exceptional richness in species. These are excellent places to explore for wild edibles, as the greater diversity often leads to more abundant foraging opportunities. National parks, wildlife refuges, and protected areas frequently fall into this category.

4. Hiking Trails and Parks: Many hiking trails and parks offer convenient and accessible locations for foraging. Trails through forests, meadows, and along rivers or lakes can lead you to an assortment of wild edibles. These spots are often well-maintained, making them accessible for beginners.

5. Rural Areas: Rural areas with less human disturbance often have bountiful foraging opportunities. Fields, woodlands, and countryside landscapes provide an array of wild plants, mushrooms, and berries.

6. Farmers' Markets and Farmers: Don't overlook the possibility of foraging close to home. Farmers' markets and local farmers can be excellent sources of information on where you might find wild edibles on their land or in nearby areas. Some may even allow foraging on their properties with permission.

7. Beachcombing: Coastal areas, such as beaches and rocky shorelines, offer a unique opportunity for foraging. Seaweeds, edible beach greens, and even shellfish can be found along the coast. Be mindful of local regulations and any restrictions on harvesting.

8. Know Your Seasons: Different wild edibles are in season at various times of the year. Research and observation will help you identify the prime time for specific foraging excursions. Early spring may be perfect for wild garlic, while late summer could yield an abundance of wild berries.

9. Learn to Read the Landscape: Developing the ability to read the landscape is essential. Pay attention to the types of vegetation, the presence of water sources, and the various ecosystems that you encounter. Different plants thrive in different conditions, and a discerning eye can lead you to potential foraging sites.

10. Responsible Foraging: Always practice ethical foraging principles. This includes obtaining any necessary permits or permissions, adhering to harvesting regulations, and respecting the environment. Overharvesting, especially in sensitive ecosystems, can harm both the environment and future foragers.

11. Start in Your Backyard: Foraging doesn't always require traveling great distances. Start by identifying what's available in your own backyard, garden, or nearby green spaces. You might be surprised by the abundance of wild edibles close to home.

12. Join Foraging Groups: Local foraging groups and clubs can provide a wealth of information and connections. Group members often share their favorite foraging spots and welcome newcomers to the world of wild edibles.

Finding suitable foraging locations is a thrilling exploration in itself. It's a journey that requires an intimate understanding of the environment, a keen eye for detail, and a commitment to sustainable and ethical practices. As you hone your skills and become familiar with the ecosystems around you, you'll discover that the world is a vast and inviting pantry, waiting to be explored and savored.

CHAPTER THREE

Edible Treasures of the Wild

In a world where the supermarket shelves overflow with neatly packaged and homogenized foods, and our connection to the natural world is increasingly distant, there is a profound and primal yearning to rediscover the edible treasures that nature offers. The wilderness, whether it be a sprawling forest, a meandering riverbank, or a windswept coastline, teems with a secret bounty that has sustained humans for millennia. This hidden realm of nourishment and wonder, concealed amidst the foliage, beneath the soil, and beneath the waters, is the subject of our exploration—Edible Treasures of the Wild.

As modern life races forward with its conveniences and processed foods, there is an essential need to return to the roots of our sustenance. We find ourselves longing for a more profound connection to the land and a reverence for the food it offers, a connection that has been forged through countless generations of foragers, gatherers, and hunters. This connection to the wild is not a mere journey for sustenance but an exploration of the essence of life itself—a journey to the heart of our ancestral past and a vibrant celebration of the ecosystems that continue to sustain us.

Edible Treasures of the Wild invites you to embark on a captivating voyage into the untamed world. It is a journey where you will become an apprentice of the wild, learning the secrets of nature's pantry. In the act of foraging, you will step into an age-old practice that kindles the spirit of adventure and invites you to experience the world with new eyes, attuned to the hidden gems that nature provides.

This book is your compass and guide as you navigate the intricate and diverse landscape of wild edibles. From lush meadows adorned with vibrant wildflowers to ancient forests adorned with mushrooms, each chapter unfolds the story of nature's bounty, introducing you to the edible treasures it holds. You will become acquainted with an array of plants, fungi, herbs, and even seaweeds, each offering its unique flavors, nutritional benefits, and the enchanting lore that surrounds it.

Edible Treasures of the Wild is more than just a compendium of botanical knowledge; it is an invitation to become a custodian of the land. Foraging is not merely about taking from the environment; it is a reciprocal exchange, a dance with nature that involves giving back as much as we receive. It is a practice that imparts the wisdom to respect the rhythms of the seasons, to nurture the ecosystems that sustain us, and to partake in the time-honored tradition of ethical and sustainable foraging.

As we embark on this foraging odyssey, you will learn to distinguish edible treasures from their potentially toxic counterparts, practice sustainable foraging, and understand the myriad benefits that this ancient art offers. Through the guidance of experienced foragers and naturalists, you will gain insight into the essence of responsible gathering and the joy that comes from a profound connection with the wild.

The chapters that follow will lead you through the verdant landscapes, across the shores, and beneath the canopies, offering a diverse array of edible wonders for your exploration. The exploration takes us to the world of wild salads, herbal infusions, and succulent berries, allowing you to become a culinary artist in your own right. You will uncover the alchemical secrets of preservation, mastering the art of drying, freezing, and canning, ensuring that the flavors of the wild remain within reach throughout the seasons.

Edible Treasures of the Wild is an ode to the timeless art of foraging. It is a love letter to the natural world, beckoning us to rekindle our bond with the land and celebrate the myriad flavors, nutrients, and stories that it has to offer. The wild is not just a source of nourishment; it is a wellspring of inspiration, a sanctuary for the spirit, and a testament to the interconnectedness of all life on Earth.

So, let us embark on this enchanting journey to unveil the edible treasures of the wild. Together, we will delve into the heart of the wilderness, guided by knowledge, curiosity, and a reverence for the Earth. This is your invitation to nourish both body and soul, to savor the delectable gifts that nature bestows upon us, and to forge a deeper connection with the world around us. Welcome to the world of Edible Treasures of the Wild, where the land itself becomes your provider, your mentor, and the eternal source of wonder and sustenance.

Wild Plants: A Bounty of Nutrient-Rich Greens

In our modern world, where supermarkets are brimming with cultivated produce, it's easy to forget that there is a treasure trove of nutrient-rich greens waiting to be discovered in the wild. Wild plants, often deemed as weeds, are a hidden bounty of exceptional nutritional value, tantalizing flavors, and culinary versatility. Foraging for wild plants is not only a journey of reconnection with nature but also a quest for vibrant health through the consumption of these often-overlooked botanical marvels.

Diversity of Wild Greens

Wild plants come in an astounding array of forms, colors, and flavors. From the delicate, tender leaves of early spring to the robust, hardy greens that withstand the rigors of winter, wild plants offer a rich tapestry of flavors and nutrients. Among the most sought-after wild greens are:

1. Dandelion (Taraxacum officinale): Perhaps one of the most recognizable and abundant wild greens, dandelions are packed with vitamins and minerals. Their peppery leaves are a delightful addition to salads or can be sautéed as a side dish.

2. Purslane (Portulaca oleracea): With its succulent leaves and a lemony flavor, purslane is a nutritional powerhouse, rich in omega-3 fatty acids, vitamins, and antioxidants. It can be enjoyed fresh or lightly cooked.

3. Lamb's Quarters (Chenopodium album): Often referred to as wild spinach, lamb's quarters have leaves similar in taste and texture to cultivated spinach. They are a superb source of vitamins A and C, as well as minerals.

4. Wild Garlic (Allium ursinum): This aromatic wild plant imparts a gentle garlicky flavor and is rich in vitamins, particularly vitamin C. It can be used fresh in salads or cooked into soups, sauces, and pestos.

5. Nettles (Urtica dioica): Though they have stinging hairs, nettles are highly nutritious, containing iron, calcium, and vitamins A and C. Cooking or drying neutralizes their stings, allowing them to be used in teas, soups, and sauces.

6. Chickweed (Stellaria media): Chickweed is known for its mild, slightly sweet flavor and high vitamin and mineral content. It can be eaten fresh in salads or used as a garnish.

7. Plantain (Plantago major): Not to be confused with the banana-like fruit, plantain leaves are edible and packed with vitamins, especially vitamin K. They have a slightly bitter flavor and are best used in salads or cooked dishes.

Nutritional Value

Wild plants are nutritional powerhouses, often surpassing their cultivated counterparts. They are abundant sources of vitamins, minerals, and antioxidants. Many wild greens are particularly high in vitamin C, an essential nutrient for a healthy immune system. For example, dandelion leaves contain more vitamin A and C than cultivated spinach. Wild plants are also rich in vitamin K, essential for bone health and blood clotting, with notable examples being lamb's quarters and plantain leaves.

Minerals are abundant in wild plants, as well. Purslane, for instance, is an excellent source of magnesium and calcium. Nettles provide ample iron and calcium, while chickweed offers potassium.

Health Benefits

The consumption of wild plants brings a host of health benefits. Not only are they rich in essential nutrients, but many also possess medicinal properties. For instance, nettles are known for their anti-inflammatory and diuretic effects, making them useful for conditions like arthritis and high blood pressure.

Wild plants often contain antioxidants that help protect cells from oxidative stress, reducing the risk of chronic diseases. The diverse array of compounds in wild greens supports overall health and well-being.

Culinary Delights

In addition to their nutritional value, wild plants add a culinary dimension to your meals. They offer a burst of fresh, seasonal flavors that range from peppery to tangy, and they can be incorporated into a variety of dishes. Wild greens can be used in salads, as ingredients in soups and stews, or as garnishes for main courses. Some can even be used in teas or as a filling for pies.

Sustainable and Ethical Foraging

Foraging for wild plants is not just about reaping the benefits of nature but also about being a responsible steward of the environment. Sustainable foraging practices, such as selective harvesting and the leave-no-trace principle, are essential to ensure that the wild greens continue to thrive.

Ethical foraging means understanding the ecosystems from which we gather and respecting the natural balance. It involves avoiding overharvesting and protecting the habitats where wild plants grow.

Safety First

While the world of wild plants is brimming with culinary delights and health benefits, safety is paramount. Ensuring proper identification is crucial to avoid confusion with potentially toxic look-alikes. It's imperative to learn from experienced foragers, consult field guides, and, when in doubt, refrain from consuming wild plants until their identity is confirmed.

Edible treasures of the wild offer a gateway to both culinary adventure and a deeper connection with nature. These often-underappreciated greens invite us to step outside, explore our natural surroundings, and rediscover the enchanting world of wild plants. By responsibly foraging for these nutrient-rich greens, we not only nourish our bodies but also renew our reverence for the land and its generous offerings. The wild, it turns out, is a flourishing garden of health and flavor, waiting to be explored and embraced.

Nuts, Berries, and Fruits: Nature's Sweet Treats

The luscious sweetness of ripe berries, the satisfying crunch of freshly cracked nuts, and the succulence of tree-ripened fruits are some of nature's most delectable gifts. While often enjoyed as snacks or ingredients in culinary creations, these treasures from the natural world offer much more than their delightful flavors. Nuts, berries, and fruits are nutritional powerhouses, embodying the essence of health and vitality while connecting us to the rich bounty of the earth.

Nuts: Nutritional Powerhouses

Nuts are a marvel of nature, packed with essential nutrients and health benefits. From the familiar almonds, walnuts, and pecans to the exotic macadamia and Brazil nuts, each variety brings a unique blend of flavors and nutrients.

Nuts are a rich source of heart-healthy monounsaturated fats, which can help reduce bad cholesterol levels and lower the risk of heart disease. They are also dense in protein, making them a satisfying and nutritious snack. Nuts are packed with vitamins and minerals, including vitamin E, magnesium, and potassium. They are also an excellent source of antioxidants, which can help protect the body from oxidative stress and chronic diseases.

Frequently, nuts are associated with weight gain due to their calorie content. However, research suggests that the consumption of nuts does not necessarily lead to weight gain and can even help with weight management due to their satiating qualities.

Berries are renowned for their vibrant colors and sweet, tart flavors. They are rich in vitamins, particularly vitamin C, which plays a crucial role in supporting the immune system and promoting healthy skin. Berries also contain dietary fiber, which aids digestion and supports heart health. The antioxidants found in berries can protect cells from damage caused by free radicals and may reduce the risk of chronic diseases such as cancer and heart disease.

Fruits: A Cornucopia of Goodness

Fruits are perhaps the most celebrated of nature's sweet treats. They come in a dazzling variety of shapes, sizes, and flavors, from the crisp juiciness of apples to the velvety sweetness of peaches and the tropical delight of pineapples.

Fruits are brimming with essential vitamins and minerals. They are a superb source of vitamin C, which boosts the immune system, supports skin health, and aids in the absorption of iron from plant-based foods. Fruits like bananas are rich in potassium, a mineral vital for maintaining healthy blood pressure. Fruits are also a good source of dietary fiber, which helps regulate digestion, prevent constipation, and support a feeling of fullness.

Apart from being nutrient-dense, fruits also contain antioxidants that protect the body against cellular damage and inflammation. These antioxidants may help reduce the risk of chronic diseases and slow the aging process.

The Culinary Delight of Nuts, Berries, and Fruits

Nuts, berries, and fruits are not only excellent for snacking but also versatile ingredients in a wide range of culinary creations. Nuts add a delightful crunch and flavor to salads, granolas, and baked goods. They can be ground into a creamy paste to make nut butter, an excellent source of healthy fats and protein.

Berries can be used in both sweet and savory dishes. They are perfect for making jams, preserves, and pies, or for topping cereals, yogurt, and desserts. Berries also make refreshing smoothies and are often incorporated into salad dressings.

Fruits are at home in a myriad of dishes. They can be enjoyed fresh as a healthy snack or used to create mouthwatering desserts, like pies, cobblers, and fruit salads. Fruits can also be grilled to enhance their flavors or used in savory dishes, adding a touch of sweetness and depth to recipes.

Responsible Harvesting and Sustainable Practices

As with wild plants, ethical and sustainable practices are paramount when foraging for nuts, berries, and fruits. Responsible foraging means taking only what you need and ensuring that you leave the environment undisturbed. It involves respecting the habitats of these wild edibles and avoiding overharvesting.

Understanding the seasons and life cycles of these natural treasures is essential. This knowledge ensures that foragers gather when the fruits are at their peak, and it allows time for the plant to reproduce and thrive.

Safety in Foraging

While nuts, berries, and fruits are generally safe to forage, it's crucial to follow safety guidelines and employ proper identification techniques. Accurate identification is vital to distinguish between edible and potentially toxic species. As with all foraging, when in doubt, it's best to refrain from consuming anything until its identity is verified.

Nuts, berries, and fruits are not just sweet treats; they are nutritional powerhouses, bursting with flavor and health benefits. Foraging for these treasures is a joyful journey that connects us to the natural world and imparts a profound appreciation for the bounty that the earth provides. Whether enjoyed fresh or used in culinary creations, these gifts from nature enrich our lives and nourish our bodies. Their consumption is a celebration of the simple, yet profound, pleasures of nature's sweet treats.

The Art of Hunting Wild Mushrooms

Foraging for wild mushrooms is a captivating and ancient pursuit that blends elements of culinary artistry, scientific curiosity, and a deep connection to the natural world. It's a delicate dance with nature, where one must navigate the hidden realms of forests, fields, and woodlands, seeking out elusive fungal treasures. The art of hunting wild mushrooms offers not only the promise of a gourmet meal but also a profound connection to the mysteries of the forest floor.

Mycophilia: The Fascination with Mushrooms

The allure of wild mushroom foraging, known as mycophilia, has been deeply embedded in human history and cultures worldwide. This age-old practice blends reverence for nature's offerings with the thrill of uncovering hidden, often visually spectacular, fungi.

Mushrooms have an undeniable mystique. They appear in a myriad of forms, colors, and sizes, from the iconic and delectable chanterelle to the visually striking but toxic fly agaric. With a world of fungal diversity to explore, foragers often become amateur mycologists, learning to identify and understand the life cycles of various mushroom species.

The Hunt for Edibles: Choosing the Right Species

One of the essential aspects of mushroom foraging is the ability to differentiate between edible and inedible, or even toxic, species. The consequences of misidentification can be dire, making it crucial to proceed with caution and learning.

Reputable field guides, expert advice, and local knowledge are invaluable resources for novice foragers. They provide insight into the appearance, habitat, and growth patterns of edible mushrooms while also shedding light on their potentially harmful counterparts.

Popular Edible Mushrooms:

1. Morels (Morchella spp.): These distinctive, honeycomb-capped mushrooms are highly sought after for their unique flavor. They thrive in temperate forests and are a prized delicacy in many culinary traditions.

2. Chanterelles (Cantharellus spp.): Known for their apricot-like aroma, chanterelles are bright, trumpet-shaped mushrooms that are often sautéed and served with various dishes.

3. Porcini (Boletus edulis): Often called king boletes, these mushrooms have a robust, earthy flavor and are favored for their meaty texture.

4. Hen of the Woods (Grifola frondosa): This large, frilly mushroom grows in clusters, with a taste reminiscent of chicken. It is used in various dishes and vegetarian alternatives.

5. Lion's Mane (Hericium erinaceus): This distinctive, cascading mushroom resembles a lion's mane. It is celebrated for its unique texture and seafood-like flavor.

6. Oyster Mushroom (Pleurotus spp.): With a mild flavor and versatile texture, oyster mushrooms are used in a wide range of dishes.

The Rules of Responsible Foraging: Ethical and Sustainable Practices

Wild mushroom foraging extends beyond the mere collection of fungi; it involves ethical and sustainable practices. It's crucial to follow guidelines to ensure both the continued existence of these fungal wonders and the integrity of the ecosystem.

1. Leave No Trace: Foragers must minimize their impact on the environment by not damaging or disturbing the habitat, removing litter, and being aware of the ecosystems they traverse.

2. Respect Local Regulations: Some areas may have restrictions on mushroom foraging, including bans in certain parks or protected areas. Always research and adhere to local regulations.

3. Selective Harvesting: Gather only what you intend to use. Overharvesting can lead to a decline in fungal populations and is detrimental to the environment.

4. Identification Accuracy: Precise identification is paramount to ensure you gather only safe and edible mushrooms. When in doubt, do not consume any wild mushrooms.

5. No Habitat Destruction: Do not damage plants, trees, or the forest floor while searching for mushrooms. This includes avoiding trampling on delicate flora and preventing soil erosion.

Safety and Health:

While the world of wild mushroom foraging offers a thrilling journey, safety is paramount. Foragers must follow strict guidelines for accurate identification. Misidentification of toxic mushrooms can lead to serious health consequences.

Community and Sharing:

Mushroom foraging is often a communal experience, with enthusiasts sharing knowledge, locations, and even meals. Foragers often form close-knit communities, exchanging tips, techniques, and insights on fungal finds.

The art of hunting wild mushrooms takes you on a voyage through the enigmatic and captivating world of fungi. It offers more than just culinary delights; it immerses you in nature's intricacies and fosters a deep appreciation for the environment. As you learn to discern edible mushrooms from their potentially harmful counterparts, you connect with an age-old tradition, joining the ranks of those who have explored the wonders of the forest floor. With a reverence for the wild and a passion for fungi, you can unlock the secrets of this fascinating art and uncover the delights that nature provides to those who seek them.

Foraging for Seafood and Aquatic Delicacies

While the art of foraging is often associated with land-based edible treasures like wild plants and mushrooms, the bounties of nature extend far beyond the terrestrial realm. Coastal regions, freshwater habitats, and marine environments offer a plethora of seafood and aquatic delicacies waiting to be discovered by intrepid foragers. This oceanic bounty allows for a unique and adventurous approach to foraging, combining the thrill of exploration with the rewarding experience of harvesting marine flavors.

The Allure of Foraging for Seafood:

Foraging for seafood is an ancient practice that traces back to our hunter-gatherer ancestors. Coastal communities around the world have long relied on the ocean's offerings for sustenance. Today, the practice remains deeply embedded in culinary traditions, appealing to those who seek a connection to nature and a taste of the sea's riches.

The Coastal Cornucopia:

Coastal regions offer an array of seafood delights, from mollusks to crustaceans, and an abundance of edible seaweeds. These areas are particularly rich in biodiversity, making them fertile grounds for foraging. Some of the sought-after coastal treasures include:

1. Mussels and Clams: Mussels and clams can be found clinging to rocks and submerged in intertidal zones. They are a source of protein and rich in vitamins and minerals. These bivalves are often used in soups, stews, or enjoyed with a simple white wine and garlic sauce.

2. Oysters: Oysters are prized for their briny, oceanic flavor. They are typically found attached to rocks or in oyster beds.

They are often served raw or cooked in a variety of preparations.

3. Crabs: Crabs can be found scuttling along coastlines and in tidal pools. They are a rich source of lean protein and can be used in a myriad of dishes, including crab cakes and seafood soups.

4. Seaweeds: Seaweeds such as nori, dulse, and kelp are rich in vitamins and minerals and are used in a variety of culinary applications, from sushi wraps to salads.

Freshwater Foraging

Freshwater environments also offer a cornucopia of aquatic delicacies. Rivers, lakes, and streams are teeming with fish, crayfish, freshwater mussels, and edible aquatic plants. The act of angling for fish or catching crayfish is a popular form of freshwater foraging. However, it's crucial to be mindful of local regulations, as these may vary from one region to another.

Ethical and Sustainable Foraging Practices:

Foraging for seafood and aquatic delicacies carries with it a unique set of responsibilities and considerations. Ethical and sustainable foraging practices are vital to ensure the continued health of aquatic ecosystems and the conservation of these valuable resources.

1. Respect Catch Limits: Adhere to local catch limits and regulations. These rules are in place to protect the sustainability of aquatic species and to prevent overharvesting.

2. Preserve Ecosystems: Be mindful of the ecosystems you are foraging from. Avoid damaging fragile habitats, and leave no trace of your presence. Tread lightly and protect the environment that provides you with these natural treasures.

3. Selective Harvesting: Gather only what you need and can use. Overharvesting can harm both the environment and future foragers.

4. Proper Identification: Precise identification of species is paramount, especially when foraging for seafood. Misidentification can lead to the consumption of potentially harmful or protected species.

Safety and Health:

Foraging for seafood requires particular attention to safety and health. Accurate identification of species is crucial to prevent harmful encounters. It's essential to recognize potential hazards, such as shellfish toxins, and to know which parts of a species are edible.

Community and Sharing:

Foraging for seafood often fosters a sense of community among enthusiasts. Sharing knowledge, locations, and even recipes is a common practice. Coastal and freshwater foragers frequently come together to celebrate the bounties of the sea and freshwater through seafood festivals and gatherings.

The Thrill of Exploration:

Foraging for seafood and aquatic delicacies is an adventurous pursuit that offers a profound connection to the natural world. It enables foragers to explore coastlines, riversides, and aquatic ecosystems, immersing themselves in the diverse and fascinating world of marine and freshwater life. The act of foraging for seafood not only rewards the palate with flavors of the sea but also grants foragers a sense of reverence for the ocean's and freshwater's treasures.

Foraging for seafood and aquatic delicacies is a unique way to connect with the bounties of the natural world, providing a delightful blend of culinary adventure, sustainable practices, and the joys of exploring coastal and freshwater habitats. It celebrates the art of responsible foraging, inviting us to savor the freshest flavors the waters have to offer while cherishing the ecosystems that provide us with such oceanic delights.

CHAPTER FOUR

From Forest to Table: Preparing and Preserving Your Foraged Finds

In a world where the supermarket aisles are laden with packaged and processed foods, there is a growing yearning for a more profound connection with the sources of our sustenance. From the forests, meadows, and coastlines to the freshwater streams and gardens, the bounty of nature beckons us to return to the roots of our food, to forage for the treasures hidden amidst the foliage, below the soil, and beneath the waters. "From Forest to Table: Preparing and Preserving Your Foraged Finds" is an exploration of the art and science of transforming nature's offerings into culinary delights that grace our tables.

The act of foraging is a journey of rediscovery—a quest that leads us back to our ancestral past when humans were intimately connected with the land, its flora, and fauna. It is an invitation to explore the hidden wonders of nature's pantry and an opportunity to regain the wisdom to not only harvest the wild but also to cherish, honor, and preserve it for generations to come.

The Heart of Foraging:

Foraging embodies a timeless art that transcends cultures, generations, and geography. From indigenous peoples who have sustained themselves on the wilds of the land for millennia to modern foragers who are inspired by the desire to connect with the natural world, foraging is a celebration of the land's offerings and a testament to our interconnectedness with the environment.

"From Forest to Table" is your guide through this extraordinary journey, from the very first moment you set foot in the wilderness, through the act of harvesting the freshest of finds, to the art of preparing them in a way that preserves their natural essence and culinary potential. This book serves as both a compass and a mentor, offering knowledge and insights on the multifaceted aspects of foraging.

The Culinary Exploration:

Beyond the thrill of discovery and the satisfaction of a successful foraging excursion lies the culinary delight of transforming your wild finds into exquisite dishes. With "From Forest to Table," you will become an alchemist in the kitchen, crafting creations that showcase the unique flavors, textures, and nutritional benefits of the wild ingredients you have gathered.

Each chapter in this book unveils the secrets of the wild, introducing you to a diverse array of ingredients—from wild plants and mushrooms to nuts, berries, seafood, and aquatic delicacies. You will learn to appreciate the distinct characteristics of each component, enabling you to turn them into culinary masterpieces.

Preservation as a Timeless Skill:

The art of preserving your foraged finds is a cornerstone of "From Forest to Table." In the cycle of the seasons, foraged treasures come and go, yet their flavors can be enjoyed year-round through the alchemy of preservation. Discover the ancient techniques and modern methods of drying, freezing, canning, fermenting, and pickling, allowing you to savor the essence of the wild, even during the coldest winter months.

Sustainable and Ethical Foraging:

Ethical and sustainable foraging is an integral part of the forager's code. "From Forest to Table" offers insight into responsible harvesting, teaching you to ensure the well-being of the ecosystems that provide for you and the generations to come. Learn how to tread lightly on the land, respect local regulations, and leave no trace of your foraging activities.

The Safety of the Wild:

Your safety and well-being are paramount. The book emphasizes the importance of accurate identification and knowledge to distinguish between edible treasures and potentially harmful species. The world of foraging is enchanting, but it comes with its unique set of considerations. Foraging for your finds brings with it a profound sense of connection, a treasure hunt for the senses, and an opportunity to participate in an age-old tradition.

"From Forest to Table: Preparing and Preserving Your Foraged Finds" is an invitation to savor the gifts of the wild, to connect with the natural world, and to explore the ageless art of foraging. It is an homage to the world's pantries, hidden amidst the forests, meadows, and coastal landscapes. This book is an ode to the time-honored practice of ethical and sustainable foraging and an opportunity to savor the flavors, stories, and wonders that nature bestows upon us. As you embark on this journey, you will discover that the wilderness is not merely a source of nourishment but a wellspring of inspiration, offering its treasures to those who seek to return to the roots of their food and find sustenance and joy "From Forest to Table."

Harvesting Techniques for Various Plants and Foods

The art of harvesting is a crucial skill in the world of foraging and agriculture. Understanding when and how to gather plants and foods is essential to ensure not only the best possible quality but also the long-term health and sustainability of ecosystems. Different plants and foods require specific techniques for successful and responsible harvesting, and mastering these methods is key to both honoring the land and enjoying the benefits of a bountiful harvest.

Wild Plants:

Foraging for wild plants is a delicate and sustainable practice. It involves collecting a diverse array of edible treasures, including greens, herbs, roots, and fruits, from their natural habitats. Here are some common techniques for harvesting wild plants:

1. Gentle Picking: Many wild plants, especially leafy greens, can be harvested by gently plucking the leaves or stems. Use your fingers or small hand pruners to ensure minimal damage to the plant.

2. Root Harvesting: When harvesting root vegetables like wild carrots or dandelion roots, use a digging stick or a small trowel to carefully unearth the plant. Be mindful not to damage the surrounding plants or the root itself.

3. Cutting: For tall plants or woody herbs, such as wild asparagus or rosemary, use sharp scissors or pruning shears to make clean cuts. This method allows you to gather the desired parts while leaving the rest of the plant intact for future growth.

4. Berry Picking: When collecting wild berries, it's best to use your fingers or a small basket to gently pick the fruits, ensuring that they remain intact. Avoid crushing or bruising the berries to preserve their quality.

5. Leave No Trace: An essential practice in wild plant harvesting is the "leave no trace" principle. Minimize your impact on the environment by avoiding trampling on other plants or disturbing the habitat. Harvest no more than you need, ensuring the continued health of the plant population.

Cultivated Plants:

Cultivated crops offer a predictable source of food, but proper harvesting techniques are still essential to ensure the best quality and yield. Here are some methods for harvesting commonly cultivated plants:

1. Herbs: Harvest herbs by snipping the leaves or stems, typically in the morning when their flavor is most concentrated. Use sharp scissors or pruners to make clean cuts just above a leaf node to encourage new growth.

2. Leafy Greens: Harvest leafy greens like lettuce, spinach, and kale by cutting the outer leaves with scissors or a knife, allowing the inner leaves to continue growing. Regular harvesting promotes a steady supply of fresh greens.

3. Root Vegetables: Gently dig around the root with a fork or your hands to loosen the soil before lifting the vegetable.

Be careful not to damage the roots, as this can reduce their quality and shelf life.

4. Tomatoes: When harvesting tomatoes, grasp the fruit firmly and twist it gently to separate it from the plant. This method helps prevent damage to both the fruit and the plant.

5. Fruit Trees: When collecting fruits from trees, use a ladder or a fruit-picking pole to reach higher branches. Handle the fruits carefully to avoid bruising and damaging the tree's limbs.

Aquatic Foods:

Harvesting seafood and aquatic delicacies, such as fish, shellfish, and seaweeds, requires specific techniques that vary depending on the type of food source. Here are some common methods for collecting aquatic foods:

1. Fishing: Fishing involves using various tools, including fishing rods, nets, and traps, to catch fish. The technique depends on the fish species and local regulations. It's essential to follow catch limits and respect waterway guidelines.

2. Shellfish Gathering: Collecting shellfish like clams, mussels, and oysters typically involves digging or prying them from their habitats. Be aware of local regulations and harvesting seasons to ensure sustainability.

3. Seaweed Harvesting: Seaweeds can be hand-harvested or cut from rocks using specialized knives or scissors. Ensure that you have accurate identification to avoid collecting toxic species. Harvest only what you need and leave the environment undisturbed.

Preservation:

After harvesting, it's often necessary to preserve the foods for future consumption. Techniques such as drying, freezing, canning, fermenting, and pickling are used to ensure the freshness and longevity of the harvest.

Each preservation method depends on the type of food and personal preferences. Drying herbs, for example, involves hanging them in a well-ventilated area, while freezing might require blanching vegetables before storing them in the freezer. Canning involves sealing foods in jars, while fermentation and pickling rely on preserving through the fermentation process and the use of brine or vinegar.

In the world of foraging and agriculture, mastering harvesting techniques is as important as knowing what to collect. Proper harvesting not only ensures the highest quality and flavor of foods but also promotes the long-term health of ecosystems. Responsible and sustainable harvesting practices protect the environment, enabling future generations to enjoy the same natural abundance. Whether you're collecting wild plants, cultivated crops, or aquatic delicacies, understanding the right techniques is essential for both honoring the land and enjoying a bountiful and wholesome harvest.

Cleaning and Storing Your Foraged Bounty

Once you've embarked on a successful foraging adventure and harvested a bountiful collection of wild plants, mushrooms, nuts, berries, or other delights from nature's pantry, your journey is far from over. Properly cleaning and storing your foraged bounty is an essential step in preserving the quality, flavor, and nutritional value of these precious finds. With the right techniques and a touch of care, you can savor the taste of the wild year-round while ensuring that the environment and your health are respected.

The Importance of Cleaning:

Cleaning is the first and critical step in the post-harvest process. Wild-gathered foods are exposed to various elements, including soil, insects, and sometimes even pollution. Cleaning helps remove these contaminants and ensures that what you consume is safe and free from impurities. Here are some tips for cleaning your foraged bounty:

1. Inspect and Discard: Before cleaning, inspect your harvest carefully. Discard any items that show signs of spoilage, damage, or contamination. Pay attention to any visible insects or dirt.

2. Rinse and Soak: In general, the first step in cleaning is to rinse your foraged foods under cool, running water. Use a gentle stream to avoid bruising delicate items. For fruits and vegetables, you can also soak them briefly in water to loosen dirt and insects. However, be cautious not to oversoak, as some fruits and mushrooms can become waterlogged and lose their texture.

3. Use a Soft Brush: For mushrooms, particularly those with intricate gills, a soft brush can be handy. Gently brush away any dirt or debris without damaging the delicate structures.

4. Pat Dry: After rinsing, pat your foraged items dry with paper towels or a clean kitchen cloth. This step is essential to remove excess moisture, which can lead to spoilage during storage.

5. Inspect Again: After cleaning, give your items another quick inspection to ensure that they are free from contaminants. Look for any remaining dirt, insects, or damaged portions that may have been missed during the initial cleaning.

Storage Techniques:

Proper storage is the key to preserving the flavor and nutritional value of your foraged bounty. Different foods require different storage methods to maintain their freshness. Here are some guidelines for storing your foraged finds:

1. Refrigeration: Many fruits, vegetables, and greens should be stored in the refrigerator to extend their shelf life. Store them in perforated plastic bags or airtight containers to maintain humidity and freshness.

2. Drying: For herbs, mushrooms, and some fruits, drying is a traditional and effective preservation method. Air-drying or using a dehydrator can help reduce moisture content and extend the shelf life. Once dried, store in airtight containers in a cool, dark place.

3. Freezing: Some foods, like berries and certain vegetables, can be preserved by freezing. Blanch vegetables before freezing to prevent spoilage, and ensure that your items are well-sealed in freezer-safe bags or containers.

4. Canning: Canning is a popular method for preserving fruits and vegetables. Properly sterilized jars and lids are filled with the food, sealed, and processed in a boiling water bath or pressure canner, depending on the acidity of the item. Canned foods can be stored in a cool, dark place.

5. Fermentation: Fermentation is a preservation method for items like cucumbers, cabbage, and even wild mushrooms. The process involves creating a brine with salt and water, allowing beneficial bacteria to convert sugars into lactic acid. Once fermented, items can be stored in the refrigerator.

Labeling and Organization:

To avoid confusion and ensure you use your foraged bounty before it loses freshness, labeling and organization are key. Use labels to indicate the type of food, the date of harvest, and any specific notes about its condition. Keep your storage area well-organized to help you locate items easily.

Safety and Health:

When it comes to cleaning and storing foraged foods, safety and health are of utmost importance. Take care to avoid cross-contamination between different items. Wash your hands thoroughly and ensure that all equipment and surfaces are clean and sanitized. Additionally, proper identification of foraged items is crucial to avoid consuming toxic or harmful species.

The Joy of Savoring the Wild:

Cleaning and storing your foraged bounty allows you to extend the joy of your foraging adventure throughout the seasons. Whether you're preserving the essence of the wild through drying and canning or enjoying the fresh harvest from your refrigerator, the effort is well worth it. Properly cleaned and stored foraged items will bring the taste of the wild to your table, connecting you to the land and celebrating the rich flavors of nature's pantry.

Culinary Adventures: Cooking with Foraged Ingredients

The heart of foraging is the thrill of discovering nature's hidden treasures and the joy of savoring their unique flavors. But what truly elevates the foraging experience is the art of transforming these wild finds into delectable dishes that grace your table. Cooking with foraged ingredients is a culinary adventure that awakens your senses and connects you to the land in a profound way. It's a journey that involves creativity, resourcefulness, and a deep appreciation for the richness of the natural world.

The Culinary Palette of Foraged Ingredients:

Foraged ingredients offer a diverse and exotic palette for culinary exploration. From wild plants and mushrooms to nuts, berries, and edible flowers, the possibilities are endless. Each ingredient brings its own distinct flavors, textures, and stories from the wild. Some of the most popular foraged ingredients include:

1. Wild Mushrooms: The world of wild mushrooms offers a fascinating range of flavors, from the earthy richness of morels to the nutty notes of chanterelles and the umami intensity of porcini. These mushrooms are often featured in hearty stews, savory tarts, or sautéed to perfection.

2. Wild Greens: Foraged greens like dandelion, purslane, and lamb's quarters can be used in salads, pestos, or sautéed as a flavorful side dish. Their bitter and peppery notes add depth to various dishes.

3. Berries: Wild berries, such as blackberries, raspberries, and blueberries, are prized for their sweetness and are perfect for pies, jams, and desserts. They can also be used in savory dishes to add a touch of tartness.

4. Nuts: Foraged nuts like acorns, chestnuts, and hickory nuts bring a satisfying crunch to recipes. They can be roasted, ground into flour, or incorporated into both sweet and savory dishes.

5. Edible Flowers: Flowers like violets, nasturtiums, and borage provide a burst of color and subtle floral flavors to salads, garnishes, and cocktails.

Cooking Techniques:

Cooking with foraged ingredients often requires creativity and adaptability. Different ingredients may need various cooking techniques to showcase their flavors and textures. Here are some cooking methods to consider:

1. Sautéing: Sautéing is a versatile method for cooking wild mushrooms, greens, and nuts. It allows you to concentrate flavors and create delicious, caramelized surfaces.

2. Roasting: Roasting intensifies the flavors of foraged ingredients, such as root vegetables or nuts. It brings out their natural sweetness and adds depth to the dish.

3. Baking: Wild berries and fruits are excellent for baking into pies, muffins, and crisps. Their natural sweetness pairs perfectly with buttery pastry and crumbly toppings.

4. Pickling and Fermenting: Pickling and fermenting are techniques often used to preserve foraged items like wild ramps, cucumbers, or garlic scapes. They add complexity and tangy notes to various dishes.

5. Infusions: Edible flowers and aromatic herbs can be used to create infused oils, vinegars, and syrups, adding unique and delightful flavors to dressings, cocktails, and desserts.

Safety and Identification:

Proper identification of foraged ingredients is paramount to ensure that what you are cooking with is safe to eat. Misidentifying wild plants or mushrooms can have serious health consequences. It's essential to rely on reputable field guides, expert advice, and local knowledge when identifying and collecting foraged items. If you're uncertain about an ingredient, it's best to refrain from using it until its identity is verified.

Ethical Harvesting and Sustainability:

Incorporating ethical and sustainable practices into your foraging adventure is part and parcel of the culinary journey. Responsible harvesting ensures that ecosystems are not damaged or overharvested. It includes respecting the habitats of these wild edibles and leaving no trace of your presence.

The Joys of Culinary Foraging:

Cooking with foraged ingredients is a celebration of the land and the incredible flavors it provides. It's an invitation to explore the world of wild foods and create dishes that honor their unique characteristics. Foraging for wild ingredients fosters a deep connection to nature, allowing you to appreciate the bounty of the natural world in a way that few culinary experiences can match.

Whether you're a seasoned forager or a beginner just beginning your culinary adventure, cooking with foraged ingredients offers an unparalleled opportunity to engage with the land, celebrate the changing seasons, and discover the delightful surprises nature has to offer. The resulting dishes are not just about flavors; they are a reflection of the environment, a testament to the creativity of the cook, and a true embodiment of the forager's spirit.

Drying, Freezing, and Canning for Year-Round Enjoyment

The rewards of foraging often come in seasonal bursts, with the natural world offering up its bounties during specific times of the year. To extend the pleasure of foraged finds beyond their brief availability, it's essential to master the art of preservation. Drying, freezing, and canning are three key techniques that allow you to enjoy the flavors of the wild throughout the year, ensuring your pantry remains stocked with nature's delights, even when the world outside is barren.

Drying: Capturing the Essence of the Wild

Drying is one of the oldest and simplest methods of preserving food, and it's a particularly effective technique for many foraged ingredients. The process of drying removes the moisture from the food, thereby inhibiting the growth of bacteria and microorganisms that lead to spoilage. Here's how to harness the power of drying for year-round enjoyment:

1. Preparation: Start by cleaning and inspecting your foraged items. Remove any damaged or unripe portions. For fruits, slice them into even pieces. For herbs and mushrooms, arrange them on drying racks.

2. Air Drying: Many foraged herbs and mushrooms can be air-dried. Simply hang them in small bundles or lay them out on screens or trays in a well-ventilated area, away from direct sunlight. Make sure they are spaced apart to allow proper air circulation.

3. Oven Drying: An oven can be used for more controlled drying. Place your foraged ingredients on baking sheets in a single layer and set your oven to the lowest possible temperature, often around 140-160°F (60-70°C). Leave the oven door slightly ajar to facilitate moisture escape.

4. Dehydrator: A food dehydrator is a fantastic tool for efficient drying. It provides consistent, low-temperature airflow, which is ideal for preserving the flavors of your foraged finds.

5. Storing Dried Goods: Once your items are fully dried, store them in airtight containers in a cool, dark place. Glass jars or vacuum-sealed bags work well for this purpose. Properly dried items can last for many months, if not years.

Freezing: Nature's Bounty in the Deep Freeze

Freezing is a superb preservation technique for a wide range of foraged ingredients, especially those that contain high water content. This method involves reducing the temperature of the food to below freezing, effectively halting the growth of bacteria and enzymes. Here's how to make the most of your freezer for year-round foraging enjoyment:

1. Cleaning and Blanche: Clean your foraged finds and blanch them briefly in boiling water This step helps to preserve the color, flavor, and texture of the items. After blanching, shock them in ice water to stop the cooking process.

2. Drain and Dry: After blanching, drain your items thoroughly and pat them dry with paper towels. This helps to remove excess moisture, which can lead to freezer burn.

3. Portion and Package: Divide your items into portion sizes suitable for your needs. Use airtight freezer bags or containers, removing as much air as possible to prevent freezer burn. Label the packages with the contents and the date to ensure you can easily identify them later.

4. Flash Freezing: Some items, like berries, can be flash-frozen on a baking sheet before transferring them to bags or containers. This method keeps them from sticking together in a clump.

5. Temperature Control: Maintain your freezer at a consistent temperature of 0°F (-18°C) or lower. This ensures that your foraged items remain in optimal condition for extended periods.

Canning: A Taste of Summer All Year Long

Canning is a time-honored method of preserving foraged finds, allowing you to create sealed jars of your favorite fruits, vegetables, and even pickles. Canning can be done using two methods: water bath canning and pressure canning. The method you choose depends on the acidity of the food you're preserving. Here's how to make the most of canning for year-round enjoyment:

1. Clean and Prepare: Clean your foraged items and prepare them according to your recipe. For high-acid foods, water bath canning is suitable, while low-acid foods require pressure canning.

2. Sterilize Jars and Lids: Before canning, sterilize your jars and lids by boiling them for a specified time, usually 10 minutes. Keep them hot until you're ready to fill them.

3. Pack and Process: Pack your prepared items into the sterilized jars, leaving the specified headspace. Remove any air bubbles and wipe the jar rims clean. Place the lids on top and screw on the bands.

4. Process in Boiling Water or Pressure Canner: For water bath canning, immerse the sealed jars in boiling water for the prescribed time. For pressure canning, use a pressure canner and follow the specific instructions for your food.

5. Cool and Store: After processing, allow the jars to cool on a clean, dry surface. The lids should seal with a satisfying pop, indicating that they are airtight. Store your sealed jars in a cool, dark place.

Safety and Health Considerations:

When it comes to preservation techniques like canning, safety is paramount. Follow recommended guidelines and recipes from reputable sources to ensure the safe processing and storage of your foraged finds. When canning low-acid foods, always use a pressure canner to prevent the risk of botulism.

Year-Round Enjoyment: The Fruits of Your Labor

Drying, freezing, and canning for year-round enjoyment allows you to relish the flavors of the wild at any time. These techniques ensure that the delights of foraged finds remain available even when the seasons change. Whether you're enjoying wild mushrooms in the depths of winter or savoring the taste of ripe berries in the heart of summer, preserving foraged ingredients is a culinary art that connects you to the land and celebrates the rich bounty of the natural world.

CONCLUSION

Foraging is not merely a journey into the wilderness; it's an odyssey of rediscovery, connection, and stewardship. For beginners, this age-old practice offers a doorway to the natural world, where the bounty of the land, sea, and forest awaits exploration. It's a world filled with edible treasures, from wild plants and mushrooms to nuts, berries, and aquatic delicacies, each with its unique taste and story.

Foraging also brings us back to the roots of our food, connecting us to the land and its rhythms in a way that modern supermarkets and restaurants simply cannot replicate. It's an invitation to appreciate the flavors and sustenance that nature has provided for centuries and continues to offer to those who seek it.

The journey of foraging begins with understanding essential tools, safety guidelines, and ethical considerations. It entails identifying and appreciating the rich variety of edible treasures the wild has to offer and learning to tread lightly on the land while preserving its ecosystems for future generations.

It's a journey where one learns to clean, store, and preserve the wild's riches, ensuring that the flavors of the seasons extend far beyond their natural availability. Drying, freezing, and canning become essential skills, allowing for the savoring of nature's delights even when winter's grip is tight.

The final destination of the forager's path is the kitchen, where the culinary adventure truly begins. Cooking with foraged ingredients transforms the wild finds into delectable dishes that reflect the flavors and stories of the land. It's an opportunity to create, experiment, and savor the richness of the natural world.

For beginners, foraging is a gateway to a lifelong exploration of the outdoors, a celebration of sustainable practices, and a delightful connection to the world's pantry. It's an art of discovery that encourages stewardship of the environment, ethical harvesting, and a profound respect for the wilderness.

In the end, foraging for beginners is not just about finding food; it's about finding a deeper connection to the natural world and a greater appreciation for the beauty, diversity, and abundance of our planet. It's a journey that enriches the senses, nourishes the body and soul, and instills a lasting sense of wonder and gratitude for the incredible gifts that nature bestows upon us. So, take the first step into the world of foraging, and let the adventure begin.

www.ingramcontent.com/pod-product-compliance
Lightning Source LLC
Chambersburg PA
CBHW070832260726

48660CB00005B/2022